A LONG SHOT TO

# A LONG SHOT
# TO HEAVEN

—

## JEREMY REED

THE MENARD PRESS
1982

A LONG SHOT TO HEAVEN

ISBN 0 903400 82 0

Menard Press books are distributed in North
America by SPD Inc, 1784 Shattuck Ave,
Berkeley, Cal. 94709, USA

Acknowledgements: Temenos

Cover: wood engraving 'Angel' by Willow Winston

THE MENARD PRESS
8 The Oaks
Woodside Avenue
London N12 8AR

Printed in England by
Skelton's Press Ltd
Wellingborough, Northants

# CONTENTS

I am a man of a benighted century, famished for light
and praying out of darkness in the dark.

from *Night Thoughts* by David Gascoyne

# THE ISLAND OF THE DEAD – Arnold Böcklin

Black cypresses maintain an equipoise
upon this windless isle; and those dark trees
are impenetrable of foliage,
         each sharply
delineated against a mauve sky;
and are like stalagmites grown from a sea
that's bottle-green, lit up in areas
         of translucency by the play

light from enigmatic yellow rock-zones,
imparts to brown, and ochre-veined brown stone,
of a reef on which the wiry salt grass
         is hardy,
and endures in a calm that's perennially
without season. The two have crossed alone,
the one standing at the prow's luminous;
         the oarsman in black at the stern

lets the oars stand, and shudders at the view.
It's more a homecoming for the one who's
already anticipating this reef,
         and has been
here before, and walked this rock-hewn asylum,
and heard the piano of mad Hölderlin
rise through the calm, each note a fossil-leaf
         in clarity, evoking blue

beyond a sky, that floats like a sea-pool
clouded with dark algae. Here no swallow
comes trailing sunbeams; but the island trees
         harbour rocks
that cavil for an undisclosed daybreak.
The boat is the one migrant, and gold flakes

flicker from the dripping oars. If he sees
        their forbidding arrival,

it's from a crevice, for the rock wall's blind,
and he must frame horizons in his mind
of peacock-green swept by a tail of stars.
                He came here
on a night of storm, and slept through thunder,
drugged, and confused, bundled up the rock stair
to a stone room; the light was cruel in there;
        and mesmerised, he ran around

the walls until he dropped, and awoke to
a light that wouldn't change to red, then blue,
but remained constant, a repetitious
              fixity
inside, and out; he who had loved to see
the dawn's red lava ignite treed valleys,
wondered if he'd awoken after death,
        but words came to him, poetry

from the blue spaces that the sky concealed;
and if he saw his visitant, she fled
on his awakening, and a slow oar
            trod water,
and she sat in the stern, the bright phosphor
of her figure, remaining the mirror
he contemplated with awesome terror,
        each time the words sang in his head,

and he scribbled the fragments. Words would break
at a certain pitch; and in a clear lake
he'd see the swollen rose and late pear float
          their shadows
in the clouds, and a lone swan on that pool

change from white to black. That image was cruel,
for it revealed another shore, the boat
       must have passed in its silent wake,

and with her each arrival, he would dream
of the scarlet profusion of autumn,
and wrote of his exile, the half of life,
       and ran on
down, and watched the boat put off from stone,
and would have called out, but stood there alone,
who would have wished to take her for his wife,
       certain she would never return.

## DWIGHT'S BROTHER

From that platform, his aerial survey
monitors the world's missile-corridors,
the fretwork on the screen's like coloured dye
injected for the scan of an X-ray
highlighting the brain's arteries. The sky's
a bubble policed by piranha, and we,
slow fish in a pool, ghost our cooling star

towards its extinction. Dwight lives up there,
encased in glass, his ordnance of the blue
dependent on a hair-fine sanity
he vents on me, his paralysed brother,
who read all day in a bunker, and try
to calm him on his drunken visits here.
Sometimes, he says it's happened, and we're through

with breathing, and the stratosphere's alight
with marker flares. He cracks the star bourbon
we've cased in here, and wildly flaps a ball
across a pingpong table, half the night,
and then searches the reinforced white walls
for fissures. His nervous garrulity
leaves him supine, and scarlet eyed at dawn.

Sometimes I read his private dossier,
the lethal fall out of plutonium
from failed navigational satellites,
the leakage from nuclear storage pools,
the whole pejorative ballistics threat,
and worse, his manic hypochondria,
his gnawing fear of fatal infection,

his close studies of Manson and Nixon,
the monomania that burns planets.
Often, for weeks under security,
he undergoes strict immunisation,
his brain cells made into a ziggurat
of future galaxies. His marble skin
is aerosoled to a germless comfort.

Once, lying here inside an airtight calm,
my brother's chauffeur called, an ex-Nazi
who'd undergone a sex change; he'd survived
atomic research, and the East's braindrain
prior to Nuremberg, and stayed, and danced
before my spotlight. He supported arms,
but wore delicate colours round his eyes.

Each day the sky seems nearer: what Dwight fears
are stealth aircraft who bypass detection
in their inerrable vigil over
a planet they'll ignite. No survivor
will withstand the ozoneless atmosphere,
except in these villages of bunkers
built mole-like in the earth's rotating cone.

Sometimes it catches me out: the sure hum
of the earth's spinning, and I lose control,
imagining the encompassing void,
and the red of a post-nuclear sun;
and built beneath the camp's, the tunnel road
I explore in my invalid's car when
Dwight's gone, researching reactor-vessels,

preparing for a conference. Today
I drove on in too far: the lights shut out,
and my engine went dead, while I could hear
someone running towards me, then away,
or was it the trick of a generator?
Madness, I thought, 's like a kitten at play,
it unravels the mind, until we shout,

or lose identity. And then I saw
them, huddled in a group, three who had cracked,
and taken refuge here, and claimed they were
survivors of the universal flaw.
They carried me captive through a trapdoor
to a cellar of scavengings, offal,
and on their screen the first missile attacked.

# APRIL FOOL

The big winds rapped upon our roof that night,
and hail was like glass breaking in its ping
then bouncing ricochet into white light

that sparkled with the winter's outgoing.
The first time that I rose I had hare's ears,
and moonlight travelled round me in a ring

I couldn't break the spell of. The mirror
was doing odd things on confrontation,
and was trying to exorcise a stare

that had irritated for centuries.
I felt the burden of my pendant ears
in my incomplete metamorphosis,

and the window was like a jeweller's tray
each time it crackled with frozen silver.
The moon anchored a white pearl in the bay,

and twice I rose, and twice I slept, and each
time the wind was voluble with omens:
a frog cheeped in a corner on the mat.

And then at dawn, I heard the wind abate,
red, white and cerise camellia petals
formed a sodden confetti at the gate

on which a white hare stood upon its head
mad as the month in its violent passage,
as formerly Kings trembled at the ides.

I combed my ears, and went outside to sweep
the motley leaves and petals on the lawn,
but as I walked, a dividing glass kept

me on the other side of the new day.
I saw things brightly through a looking glass;
the landscape vanished when I looked away;

and when the glass broke, I went back inside
and examined my face, (it had not changed),
I feared to show it to my waiting bride.

# THE IDES OF MARCH

They woke at the dawning of the March Ides;
the boy had loved his mother in the flesh,
and stood there, perversely dressed as the bride

he'd never be, in a black négligé,
and was to be the epicene tycoon
of their business emporium, when she

relinquished absolute power to his name.
Her head was still throbbing from the empties
that littered the persian rug, and cocaine

that had administered such lucidity,
was eroding her septum; her makeup
was a smudged confetti, and round her eyes

black rings were visible, and her debauched
son lorded it over the penthouse floor.
A cat slept on the black fourposter bed,

they'd never made it to in their drunken
passion, and had interlocked on the rug.
The windows flickered a coloured prism,

she couldn't long focus on, and a wind
was whitely frisking the double-glazing.
He disappeared, and when she turned around,

he was dressed in a toga, and his hair
glittered with pearls like Heliogabalus,
and jingling the keys to their Jaguar,

he screamed, beware the Ides of March, the Ides,
and drove off recklessly, leaving her there
to assuage wrinkles, and paint her lips red,

while he, miles distant on the motorway,
asserted speed, ignoring caveats
of an ill wind, and rejoiced in the day.

## A LONG SHOT TO HEAVEN

She reads; the faucet is the only sound,
and autumn with soft fallings tints her mind
the way red was a vein then deepened round

the yellow of a peach, and when it fell
it was ripe beyond completion. Stillness,
she thinks, is like the inside of a well –

you hear it by not knowing that it's there.
She wants to assimilate each leaf-fall,
each berry's darkening sheen, and compare

the light to clear wines, then deeper claret,
and enumerate on it in letters
shading russet sentences with regret

at his delayed homecoming. (Is it that
he's grown apart, and revoked promises)?
It is the hawthorn berry hurts her heart,

its scarlet is too bright, it has the gloss
frost sparkles with. He wasn't always there,
and once she saw him by a twisted bush

in consternation with himself, and he
was found that night unconscious in a car,
and of the event had no memory.

She writes, but feels a shadow she can't trace
pursue her thread, as though a first grey hair
kept beckoning her fingers to its place

among the brown, and in her solitaire
came the vibrant tingling of something trapped
within those facets. Was he watching her,

lost to himself again in the shadow,
his face crumpled up with unseemliness,
angrily throwing stones into that well?

## DOUBLES

It's in the apprehension that precedes
the sea bell's plaintive rocking with the swell
        that I've come to anticipate
concurrence with that other bell,
the one rung by your spirit, a tinkle,
as though flicked lightly by a budgerigar.

Tonight, I leave a light burning, and go
across the headland for the moon is full,
        and reflects in its red mirror
the fly-sized dance of my shadow.
It seems intrepid amongst those craters,
while I am fearful on these rocks below.

I know you'll ponder where my book's open
for lucubrations in these night vigils,
        linger, and leave behind a chill
I'll ascertain as you; the fall
of surf's softly diffused, the way that rain
falling on snow fields is not heard at all.

And I, walking the beach am summoned by
a watch-bell guarding the reefs with a dog's
        fidgety constancy of ear.
I shelter in a hollow crag
of rock; up there my shadow's on a peak.
How can two at such distance integrate?

Sometimes I dream of a blue lunar plain,
and how I have to cast a rope about
        the earth's diminutive spheroid,
and watch the cold light of planets
constellate space, and seeing this I fall
head-first towards our world's volcanic ball.

Beside me now, and tangibly, the sea
brings with it the spirit of great spaces,
              and is at rest from turbulence
and appetite that erases
the granite heights. I dance upon the moon
with nimble shadows of a mountain goat.

Then you, again, whom my pagoda-bell
responds to in your insubstantial flare
              of greeting as a visitant,
preoccupy. You imprint air
with the design that you have grown to be,
transparent as the ghost of a lily.

I turn my back upon that scarlet moon,
confident that my double will return,
              and sit beside my shaded lamp,
that's lit to offer asylum
to such as you. Overhead I dance on.
When I fall, how is it we measure time?

# CARTFORD

Perhaps it took minutes to register;
he daydreaming of an amanuensis
his impoverished stipend
wouldn't cater for; and he the vicar
of a wayward parish, and a bachelor
sipping sherry over a bland sermon,
he'd blotted, in the quiet of his study,
a late bee, busy at the snapdragons

in the chalk blue of the June afternoon,
while he recollected Brooke's Grantchester,
and squinted into a sunbeam
preferring to remove himself in time,
then leaving his eye search among the lime-
tree, for the song of a linnet. Perhaps
this man of the sable cloth was so far
away, dreaming of places on the map

of his native Dorset, he never heard
the abrupt expiry of an engine
overhead in the cloudless blue;
but went on listening to that jovial bird,
while a red monoplane catapulted
to wreckage, and exploded in a wood,
so that dry foliage burst into flame.
If he heard it, he never understood

its import, but mused on the green quiet
of the old walled garden. His parish seemed
docile as a centuries' old moat
in which the elder flowers were afloat
in a liquid reflection; the hamlet
as yet unthreatened by bellipotent

marauders. If he dreamed, he was startled
by distant shouts, and wondered why they lent

no urgency to his unruffled mood,
and thought it part of a dark reverie
about the cross, he'd not resolved;
and paced the garden, as one might who dreads
the advent of a terrible threshold,
and leaves that night for a distant country.
He must have left without closing the door,
and run out with his face turned to the sky:

certain it was, he never once looked back,
or was sighted. We took the remains there,
expecting his full blown cassock
to offer comfort, and bless the pieces;
the doctor distant on his country round.
Perhaps we didn't comprehend, nor he
the oddity of worse than death, who ran
away but not from our calamity.

# JOHN CLARE'S JOURNAL

Conjunctivital, lame, his nose dripping,
I teach a poor boy and refuse his coin,
and would rather have him read Thomson's Spring
than pore over figures scrawled on a slate.
Outside it rains, and my chrysanthemums,
claret, canary-yellow, white, agate,
show double flowers; and it rains
over Helpstone, and mires the country lanes.

For months, uncommonly depressed, I've sat
and watched the seasons fail, and felt a dark
oppress me, and I've stared out like a rat
from a wood-pile, terrified when I die
my sins will twist like ivy round a bark,
and leave me a lost wraith. Sometimes I cry,
and fear my family's ruin.
Everywhere the red crackle of autumn

lights brief fires; crimson hip, haw, glossy sloe,
hawthorn, and plum, black bryony berry
are winter portents, and my asters glow
in their pied embers. The same pious books
arrive from Radstock, and Taylor defers
my proofs away in London town. A rook
fares better on sparse carrion,
than I the proceeds of my rusty pen.

And still they linger, Billing's late swallows
fan the burgundy air of October
and with their late departure, I'd follow
into the blue sky, and be free. My themes
are no more fashionable than Bloomfield's were,
and he too, starved. Twice I've risen from dreams,
imagining my children laid
out as corpses by a potato spade.

And now that seasonal star, the Michaelmas
daisy, shows in blue clusters, and yellow
ruffles of chestnut leaves stipple the grass.
The little harvestbell quakes in the wind,
ragwort and marjoram linger below
the hedgerows, and twist thin threads, like my mind,
that's racked and vague. Sometimes I see
my own double madly pursuing me,

and then I cower for days in a wood,
or take to the road with gypsies, broken,
and better drunk. A poet's understood
a century too late; men badger words
into affected grace, an unspoken
eloquence, with grammar a two edged sword,
soon rusty, cast into a pool
where books are ballast for the ship of fools.

Twelve months to set a title page; small fame
for I who charm a lyric from the air,
and suffer quibbling editors who blame
me for my wrong spelling. In Lolham Lane
I found dwarf polopody, and read Blair,
and listened to the slow, fly-flashing rain
tinkle in the flood pits. Alone,
my mind becomes one with the grass and stone.

Better to be a botanist, and mark
each seasonal change, and what's peculiar
to one's native region. A huge crow carks
above me, and for three minutes I've timed
a snail's progress over a slender spar
of twig. Thirteen inches: a track aligned
without a shift to left or right:
such close-up conditions a poet's sight.

A coppled crowned crane shot at Billings pond,
a gypsy wedding over at Milton,
or a rare white maidenhair fern or frond
distracts me from the melancholy hours
I sit and ponder over Chatterton,
or muse upon the coloured plates of flowers
in Maddox's Directory –
the white peony and red anemone.

They say Byron uses a whip upon
whatever woman inspires him to verse,
and then hangs her up as a skeleton
for crows to peck. Humbled on a cart track,
my inspiration's more a wolf-eyed curse
that keeps me penniless, nosing the black
tunnels a mole snouts in my brain,
vacant for hours, and hatless in the rain.

I dreamt I died last night, or else I fled
into an unfamiliar country
enclosure had parcelled off, and instead
of finding refuge, I was hunted out,
and forced to stare into a bear's red eyes
and dance with it on a rail-line. A shout
started me, and a bailiff's grip
on my shoulder, worked up and split my lip.

I sit, tussled as my limp hollyhocks,
and watch a beggar pass. Driven from farms,
men scavenge aimlessly; the gypsies knock
and fiddle me a tune. Today I fear
a black shape that has spindle legs and arms,
and grows to envelop the sodden shire.
I am a wart between its eyes,
and yet I blow a grassblade while I cry.

# KAFKA

News came I hadn't died. Each night I'd tune
into the thin squeak of a radio,
some pirate station, or I'd pace the room,
amazed to find no stubble on my chin,
or dust mark on my impeccable suit,
attentive always to the thin shadow
that followed me, and seemed to grow
into a double, threatening with the brute
militancy of a gestapo man
who spat in my face in the street
before the frontiers closed. That night I ran,
and blood speckled my snow encrusted feet,

and a car lurched out of an alleyway,
and had me run crab-like into a maze
of streets that were invisible by day,
or which I'd circumvented all my life.
I'd often known this exit out of time,
how we sidestep the once familiar
landmarks that balance who we are
against a world of doubles, where man's wife
is man, exclusive of all loneliness,
for the flaw in our nature's sealed.
When I came to I was under duress
of strangers for a secret I concealed,

but didn't know. I escaped through a rift
in time, disquieted, and knew the blaze
of my own race burning. Human ash sifts
through every breath expelled. Tonight I hear
police klaxons wail through the deserted streets,
and listen to a censored news erase
the truth, and watch my shadow raise

a troubled finger. It's I who retreat,
and leave my double behind bolt and chain
to fatten on my residue.
Outside an armoured car sidles the rain.
Twenty years on, it will be déjà vu.

## STEPPING STONES

On stepping stones beside a lily pond,
they paused, uncertain of their love as steps
taken from here. Neither would turn around

though both needed assurance of clasped hands;
and somewhere in the Turner kingfisher
of that reflected sky, a violet band

of storm buzzed; a bee in a snapdragon
audibly somnolent was all it seemed.
She wondered too of the parochial banns,

that proclamation to be honoured or
contended by some stranger's arrival
who'd watched her for years in a crystal ball.

They turned round. Men were bearing a coffin
over the fields, white lilies wreathed the teak;
they'd parked the hearse, and left the doors open

in the heat haze. Whatever substance filled
the divisive between two villages
seemed blown like a bird's egg; and they were chilled

by the mourners who pursued as a wake –
gin tears, and toothless mouths, and country ale.
They avowed each stayed for the other's sake,

but each was secretly frightened. The rain
was on them now, and diffused the pond's glow
from pastel to the flash of a salmon,

and when she ran ahead, she knew his face,
seen long ago at an attic window.
It was still there and waiting behind glass.

And he, she'd fled from, stood upon his stone,
quite unperturbed, then strode across the field,
and placed his strong shoulder to the coffin.

## DAYBREAK: HART CRANE

Wrongly dimensionalised, seen upside down,
the sky assumes the taunting veer of seam
that issues from a dead over's offspin.
He's outside, not behind the windowpane,

or so it seems until things stabilize
momentarily, and stubbing an empty
with clammy toes, the shock brings it all home –
the nights of orgy and the poetry

that's frozen in his mind beyond recall.
Its light is hard and refractive like frost,
and its centre is inaccessible.
He is to himself incredibly lost,

and fumbles for an unemptied tumbler,
to reassure himself with alcohol
his nerves won't jitter on Sweet's catalogue,
and hears the prostrate, dog-tired sailor roll

off the bed, and fish for his baggy pants
amongst the chaos of bedding. New York
throbs in the casement, and exchange of cars
are picking up. He bites on a cheroot,

and sneezes, feeling the old inventory
of complaints triggered off – his hay-fever
and acidosis – the bitter ground swell
of accusation in his mother's letters;

his father's defection, and looks askance
at the sailor's muscular deportment.
Often he'd been brutalized in alleys,
robbed and savaged and before the event,

but not this time. The man will go quietly
back to his ship in the Brooklyn harbour.
He looks at the disorganized papers
threshed in chaos about his typewriter,

odd phrases typed out to Sophie Tucker
on the victrola. It's his own method
of oblique strategy, a mosaic
of images to be formulated

into a poem. Left like this for weeks,
he can't return to it, or yet neglect
the nagging torment of his not writing.
He dresses slowly, and twice reselects

a choice of necktie, and the cold light hurts
his head which is engendering a phrase;
and what he scribbles while the crow cavils
are lines of what will become Paraphrase.

# EMIL OPPFER

My shoreleave means liquidation,
I come back, and Hart's sullen rage
demands excess of alcohol;
and haunted by an empty page

he jabs out incoherencies
on a typewriter, and returns
to these when sober. In the dark
I listen to shipping sirens,

and wonder at my attraction
to this man of mercurial moods
who likes to wear my sailor pants,
and rages in fierce solitude,

but importunes with me to say.
It's of the sea he wants to hear,
of the illimitable blue,
and of the discourse of sailors

bound outward into the unknown,
where only the storm-petrel dares
that wake. He'll reappear at two,
blind drunk, squinting through a cigar,

shouting out that his poet friends
need balls not the soft carpet worn
beneath a literary chair. Despair
and rage alternate with vision

of a poem he must complete,
but lacks the sustained time to do.
This raillery's customary now.
I hold him, and he sleeps a few

hours, then boils in a crucible
of insomnia, open-eyed,
pitched like a man in heavy seas
across a deck, from side to side,

who won't go down beneath the hatch.
Beside the bed, three red roses
are his one indulgent flourish.
The room's immaculate – the gloss

he keeps over his excesses.
Hart, lion of the South Street bars,
uproarious in untamed lust,
your eyes reach for the frosted stars

as though hoping assuagement's there.
Tomorrow my ship puts to sea,
where you'd follow. Ten days, ten days,
and you say that my memory

is like wine standing in a glass.
A rift is widening, so you brood,
and when you go, I read the words,
'inviolable blue latitudes

and levels of your eyes.' I pack,
and leave him money for cheroots,
and doodle anchors on my note,
press my trousers, polish my boots.

## THE VISCONTI PAPERS

A split nature's the worst divide a man
must need fashion into a unity,
so flawless must a spy's integrity
prove to the agents of a government.
And it was so with Walsingham's
caballing satellites, who'd face irons,
the rack, and thumbscrew, and spit out their teeth
rather than confess under such torment.

Today, on the steps of a gallery,
I watched a horse-chestnut split from its pod,
its mahogany-red fruit so polished,
I thought it lost pristinity of rind,
with the loss of its secrecy,
and would soon blacken underfoot, and die.
I'd met my connection inside, a man
so briefed he'd stepped out of Visconti's mind,

and interspersed the coldness of his speech
with erudite gleanings from Vasari,
a man whose unyielding formality
would pay error with a pistol's despatch.
There'd been a ministerial leak
subsequent to Visconti's last report
on the sales of British Nuclear Fuels,
I listened, then lit up a cigarette,

watching my source disappear in the Strand.
How many thus, I thought, in every street,
go anonymously about secrets.
The world's a hive in which no two bees meet
on a design both comprehend.
Babel anticipated how we'll end

in this crisis of nuclear fission.
Then I returned to thinking of the split,

and of Visconti's being twice blackmailed
for extra-ministerial scandals.
My man had no knowledge I'd fished that pool,
gone deep, and dredged one out at Bermondsey
for the white slab. The river's yield
proved the missing link to a chain I'd forged,
brightening each particle to a white glow.
I stamped on the chestnut, determinedly,

knitting my own psychic fissure thereby.
In this line, pressure is redoubtable,
and should we once crack, then our own double
is the mad automaton who will speak
without restraint, and never lie.
I looked up at the missile-policed sky;
the blue that once symbolized man's freedom,
now politically zoned, and should we breach

the wrong frontier? . . . Was Visconti alive,
or sealed inside an aluminium drum
on the sea bed? My appointment at noon
was with his former wife who'd undergone
hormone mutation. Who would grieve
if this planet became our common grave?
I lashed my car across the motorway,
resolved to drive into the ruby sun,

and not return. I had a dossier
on Visconti's retreat: a Sussex farm
where he researched into plutonium;

but I could smell a rat. The man was there –
the new officious minister
in all but name. I parked my red-hot car
a mile up the road in a clump of trees,
and got there, one hand tight on my holster:

the house was empty. Visconti was dead.
I counted the shots like birthday candles
peppering his mannequin. Broken glass
littered the converted laboratory.
A silicone breast, and a red
handbag had been discarded on the bed.
I stood a long time in the sun's last rays.
The man would be plotting to rule the sky.

# FALLING WITH THE SUN

Part of the overhang was in his hand –
    who'd gone on falling for three days,
so an observer said,
and each time it seemed he would hit the ground,
the floor of the quarry
deepened, and I followed in dread
    his falling through light without sound,

expecting somewhere, terminal bedrock,
    or black sand to withstand his fall,
then I blacked out, clinging
to roots, having once turned around in shock
and seen an iron ball
pursuing us, and its humming
    was evil; it had taken knocks,

but followed the man's falling without shift.
    Obscured by the ball, I pursued,
broke in a second man,
and when the ball veered, saw who in the shaft
fell without shift of head,
and his implacable mission,
    seemed not to dodge the ball, but drift

toward a matrix that would take his weight.
    I followed, once looking around
to see no pursuer
or tackle followed in my path. I shut
my eyes to prevent sand
rubbing, then opened to terror;
    we'd gone on falling, but the dark locked tight.

And clinging to a branch I found this man,
    who'd pursued the stone falling down,
and eluded the ball
I'd followed. He kept asking for the sun
to break through his dark dream
of falling through a shaft whose narrow walls
    were without handholds to climb up again.

I judged him delirious, but I said,
    we must have been years in falling,
and he responded, three,
without bottom. I said, look up, that red
ball which is hammering
the entrance is the sun, and we
    no choice have, but to dive in dread.

# SPOTLIGHT

The spotlight pools a mauve concentration,
and then is filtered to a softer blue,
    and we who in the darkness wait
for some tangible configuration
    to evolve from the mystery,
grow nervous, staring at the outer dark

as though it extended into all space.
I don't know why we arrived here, a car
    conveyed us through deserted streets:
I smelt the ether gag upon your face
    when I awoke, and saw the star
on the apex of the memorial

erected to the Third World War, and then
I must have slept, alike anaesthetised,
    and never knew our location,
only the darkness smelt of nasturtiums
    as church pews do, and round our heads
were bandages, and our apprehension

was of two awaiting a tribunal
to centralize beneath that violet light.
    What was before us was a hall
with staggered seating, and would a stripper
    appear when the light turned scarlet,
and discard garments on a funeral pall?

We stood, diffident, paralysed by fear,
and through the dark discerned a conference
    of military councillors,
and then the light picked out the black leather
    of someone who performed a dance,
as one might do upon the Berlin Wall

in the seconds before the shots ring out.
We watched, engrossed, as the drag dancer mimed
    decisions taken in the dark;
the connotations might have come from Brecht,
    and when I touched you, you declined
my hand, and rushed blindly for the exit.

## ACCESS TO

Your back door's access gave on to the sea;
a shocking sheer fall into grey water
a door on a precarious chain barred.
I remember how huge your cuff-links grew,
two green sea stones you'd draw up to your face
obscuring it, until their heaviness
immobilized your hands. Made them irons.
And how petrels and gulls would hourly pace
the outer walls round, and cry plangently
into blue space. I painted this as I
imagined it, but the colours washed out;
and in the centre of the empty frame
a bandaged figure spreadeagled in flight,
seemed to be gravitating up not down,
the contrary to our own compulsion.
Then in October the big winds arrived,
and the moon brought creatures from the seabed
to flap a day and night on the surface.
I painted this, and then went blindfolded,
for fear the door was open, while you chinked
your heavy wrists, and murmured, don't look down,
we're outside the door now, and can't look in.

## ODD CREATURE

Man in the garden lost his rib,
and woke that night to a red moon,
and sought his cradle in death's crib.

His opposite though similar
evoked in him a night-fever;
he felt his flesh; it bore no scar.

And recollected the green shade
preceding sleep, and then a cloud
had overcome him in the glade.

He never saw who came and went,
but pain was in his side, and who
he scented hid from his intent.

But had he lost one rib or two,
his opposite could not appease
the hunger he felt grafted to?

It seemed a third species had gone
off independently, and he
would fear its shadow in the moon.

And lived elusively; he'd hear
it in the tree-tops or its lair;
and neither would enquire for fear.

And later found its skeleton,
and dug it in the earth; it died
oddly uncontesting even

numbers, and then the two would fight,
and he would mourn its passiveness,
and she, to have known it by night.

## PRODIGAL DAUGHTER

She never found her rights of parentage,
who tried to conciliate a father
and son, and was banished to the attic,
and listened, adjudicating over
their nightly contention in secrecy,
and drank herself red-eyed to compensate
for how she couldn't lift the sacks of grain
her brothers brought from harvest. She would hide
and furtively nurture her pets, and cook,
but leave the room before their arrival.

And took to simulating how she could
exchange her identity for a man's,
and adopt her revenant brother's looks
to confuse her father's acrimony,
and connived with her estranged brother, so
that when he fled it would be for a week,
(they wouldn't search for her) and she'd maintain
his labour while their father gambled debts
to pay for native boys, and he'd return
with the law and a spade to bury him.

## PRODIGAL FATHER

You'd taken refuge on some other farm
before the one departed could return
with scars denoting electroplexy
and hands blistered from the use of a spade,
(digging graves was a form of therapy
he'd grown accustomed to, not so the means
of liquidation, nor the guards in grey
who'd forced this at the issue of a gun).
You'd known this, forcing his ostracism
deeper East than the East wall of Berlin.

And you'd hoped for anonymity there,
as a Western financier, the farm
sold off, your wife and children scavengers
across a country where troops multiplied
and foraged for crops still untouched by frost.
You'd count the money they had left in vaults,
and drink at a military headquarters,
quite certain your prodigal son was ash.
You'd sold off his possessions. When he traced
you it was armed robbery with a gun.

# LATE ONE

*In memory of Albert Collier*

Posthumously you'll have to read this one
who knew me; judiciously circumspect;
fifty years seniority when we met;
I solitary, reading Hart Crane in sea rain,

and you of the stammer, tutorial
with poetry, and reading my initial
scripts. Ostracised man of lonely rooms,
you parked your car adjacent to the sea,

routinal each day, contemplating white
Atlantic ledges, haggled with seabirds;
a foghorn plangently mewling address
of mist; then only the sleet of spindrift.

What you bequeathed was not eponymous.
It fulfilled my youthful vacuity,
those clandestine meetings; to friends you were
a life given as wholly personal.

No exactions, that rare empathy shared
by the incongruous of age. What was
intimated at was abjured against.
I still come to your parking spot, and surf

boils off the headland, turns an orange buoy
to a snorting hog. It's the sadness of
lights remembered coming on in hotels
overlooking the bay that defines grief.

You died unknown to me; a cardiac
seizure in a communal ward. I throw
a pebble down into the cliff hollow.
Its rattle seems your voice choking for words.

## BEHIND THE DOOR

And words can't grip their substance to convey
the terror of what is behind that door,
is what your blue lips intended to say,
but couldn't articulate who or why
the dark seemed pouring out of one black hole
into your head, and I would have rejoined –
words are a retriever dog set to chase
a prey it never can return with whole,
but approximate when they mean to kill,
and each time grow more enraged, more confused,
but you had taken in too much, afraid
it couldn't be dispelled, your eyes were wide
as though they'd become headlights, and the car
you stared at reduced to human pupils.
And I was tempted to say, smash the door,
and let the Dweller on the Threshold show
in all its weird malevolence, but you
were already pleading, it's gone too far,
and something beat its tail upon the floor.

## ADAM

It wasn't old age or incontinence,
the absent-mindedness to match two shoes,
or walking around unzipped worried us,
you largely housebound, but a reversion
to primordial instincts, how each day
we'd find you digging the earth with your hands
at the garden end, scooping one neat hole,
and obsessively digging until noon
made you uneasy, and you'd guard your trench,
one ear pressed to the earth as though alert
for a first seismic tremor then a split
dividing the planet in one neat line.
In time we came to forget who you were.
A father, grandfather, great grandfather,
and noticed black hair covering your skin,
coarse and hirsute as an ape, and left you
beating your tail out in the night garden,
the whole gradually unearthed, you slept out,
reading the book, shouting your name, Adam.

# CLAMP

I hear you on the other side,
angrily imploring that we
pacify your disquietude,
who were not of the natural dead,
and grow to shout about the house,
or maliciously on the road
thrust a palm against the windshield,
which grows to an enormity
causing a blackout and those deaths
we can't recall to acknowledge,
but return to recriminate
and haunt,
           so balance loses edge.

Tonight the bulbs blew, and the car
acquired a spattering of blood,
as though revealing its undercoat
for impoundment by the law;
and two were in the house, distraught,
at being denied burial,
and when I fled a giant wall
opposed me, and there was no road.

## ON THE OUTSIDE

Inured to persistent artillery,
we'd ceased to guess of the counterfeit war,
involved on sand-dunes, a perimeter-
fence gave indication to, and only boys
in search of used cartridges would trespass,
and polished these to coveted trophies.
We'd come to expect the sound of gunfire,
and didn't notice jumps between our words,
or speech hurried to a stutter when sure
of a target. It took strangers to tell
us of these oddities which had impaired
out thought and movements. When we ran we ducked.
Our village spire's regular funeral bell
went unheard in its unceasing grave toll.
And then the boys disappeared, orange flares
began to waver on our panes at night,
and a mushroom of red smoke grounded birds.
We sent out delegates, and one returned
too numb to speak and so we retreated,
finding the landscape barren, and ditches
piled with the dead, and on the road a child
brandishing a gun, commanding us back.

## BAR BOGEY

Closer too to where an acrid fire
dulls is this one, seated in a corner
of the bar, whom nothing will dispose to
speech or confraternity, nothing harrow
or mollify to expression. Someone
who seems never to have arrived or go,
to have become a distance created
by how he differentiates, to lose
himself in the consciously differing
perspectives with which others observe him,
to bend these and assimilate such search
to a contained reproval. So that when
others grew hesitant at closing time
of returning to countless lonely rooms,
and lingered, he'd become an attitude
who'd imperceptibly left, and each feared
to find him sitting in their room, and did,
and recognised how they could never hide.

## POLTERGEIST

I thought of you. The orange in my hand
became a fire with which I couldn't cope –
a fire was on my hands, you'd understand

how metaphor becomes liberally real,
and later burns would be the first issue
of how surprise is too sudden to feel.

And thinking of you brought you to the room,
you seemed estranged, and said that orange peel
was like one dead; too suddenly undone.

And later when you'd gone, the fire was me,
a fire was on my hands and in my head.
I burned an hour or more, orangely.

Translation of Genêt's

## A SONG OF LOVE

Shepherd, your sheep are frozen in cloud-snow.
Descend, and I will give you winter's fleece,
and if your sex won't warm beneath my breath,
your fragile frock will kindle to dawn's glow.

I question, is love possible at dawn?
Your song is still dormant within your throat,
although your startled face powdered with sleep
almost sung out over the white terrain.

Your charm dazzles my eye in its socket –
vessel dressed for a dark ceremony
of the Isles and night. Tall pricked, you are to me,
a black continent in isles of regret.

Wrath's golden vines induced delirium,
but anger's reprieved by your surrender,
and at your guidance the heavens wander
above us. Sleep's like putting white gloves on.

Above all, it's gentleness isolates
your delicate brow of November rain.
Your limbs carry Africa in your groin,
sinuous as the dawn serpent's grey wake.

A leaf waltzing anti-clockwise through mist,
questions on which tree you will knot your scarf? –
who stand with parted hair, part nymph, part youth
on whose harp my finger breaks the night frost.

I sport a hazel twig pinned upside down
on my cap peak, and it tickles my ear.
In a crook of your neck a bird splutters.
My horses sleep standing within a dream.

Distractedly, my eye sports with the sea,
(I wear a sandal that's wet and unstitched)
and feel my hand grow swollen and enriched
by sperm, dispensing flocks, invisibly.

Those lambs seem to graze from your hip to throat,
on a pasture that's burnished by the sun,
and flowering acacias mingle the tone
of your voice with the bee's honey-tipped note.

From their green pavillion, sea-riders
keep a constant vigil between the poles,
while you shake azure from the night's star-bowl,
and with sanded feet tread currents of air . . .

Thus nakedly ascend the blue staircase
with the vagueness of a somnanbulist
whose dreaming lips only fractionally miss
my own. The sky dissolves inside your face.

Or with your naked strength, sunder my night,
like Damien whose horses rip the deep.
Born of my own belly centaurs gallop.
I'd have a dead negro's hand shut out light.

I've garlanded those centaurs with ribbons
stolen from a girl's hair, and roses too.
Their sun drenched dresses captivatingly
made me stretch my arm out across the stream!

Always restive, your shoulder disenthralls
my hand. You who pump to my docile wrist! –
now cut my hastening hand to the quick,
agile as a thief's carmine fingernails.

In every wood and wayside, I see hands;
and at your neck a succubus has fed,
which changed into a monster of your blood,
heel in my hand; and there, a prince I found.

That smiling soldier was shot by surprise,
and on the white chalk wall his blood's trellis
still stains. Tatters of speech cling to branches,
and in the grass a hand cups rotting toes.

I speak of a country flayed to the bone.
France, with your perfumed eyes, perennially
spending your nights like us, intimately,
and O, offended France, in lover's tones.

We hear a slow ceremony of drums,
twenty, and veiled. Corpses parade the town,
while a brass cortège files beneath the moon
through wooded valleys in the late autumn.

Poor hand what dissolution! Yet you still
hop on the grass; and how can blood on stone
give birth to a page or angel of lichen
to hide me? What soldier bears your dead nails?

Unfurled from your feet is the ocean's roar?
Marvellous love story! You, a waif-child,
the sentinel of a beach, running wild,
while my amber hand attracts a devil.

And curiously asleep in his torso
lies a coiled up girl like an almond star,
and in her path blood's changed into azure.
The night's defined by a white lunar glow.

That shape becomes a rose, and purifies.
I cherish it. The night instinctively
prompts you to appear to me nakedly,
rolled up in sheets, or exposed to the skies.

But can my lip dare pluck a falling tear
from the heart of this overblown petal?
Its essence recalls a turtle dove's bell . . .
O remain a rose of perfect petal.

Spikey fruit of the sea, how your rays scratch?
But not as fiercely as the night's fine nail
picks corpses clean, which my pink tongue assails;
and if my heart in these desperate reaches,

capsizes, anchored, unable to vomit
your sex free of a harnessed sea of bile,
remember I pace motionless the while,
somewhere other than where you think I sleep.

I roll beneath a sea crowned with your wave,
labouring axles twisted by your storms;
and with a thread plucked from the horizon,
I'd climb the sky above the ocean's grave.

Or I moon hopelessly around your house,
a lame whip hanging from my neck, and see
through chinks the inexpressible beauty
of your eyes, the night will claim for palaces.

Whistle a vagrant's tune, adopt an air
that's hostile, crushing birds' nests in the grass,
I may, or whip up April clouds that pass,
carving his name with a shell on azure,

but see to it, he loses no beauty
like the fallen leaf. O my bright love-face,
night's precious star, fragile as snow or lace,
your shoulders burn in the white almond tree.

# SEAGULLS AND UFO'S

They waver indeterminate as snow
    suspended in air that resists
its downward gravity; then they scatter
frenetically into the cove below,
and home on a solitary walker
scattering bread, whose dog yelpingly frisks
even the most audacious marauder;

then hang off like cats in the interval
    preceding interlocking claws,
and hiss. Their dialect is guttural,
their accent querulously garrulous
to us who hear it from the cliff house where
we scrutinize the advancing figure
through field glasses, and hear the lag in surf

pronounce the ebb. Violet and cinnamon,
    the sky's unmoving, and the bay's
malachite. On the skyline, a freighter
laboriously slugs seaward, and thin
smoke quavers from it; sandpipers bicker
on the flats, and there a damaged bell-buoy's
stranded, its orange paint shaded to ochre,

and roughed by the big seas. The glass brings near
    a man who is incongruously
dressed in a brushed black greatcoat and bowler,
and from this distance has a demeanour
that's attentive, and not constrained by fear.
His brisk step seems to unreservedly
enforce the conviction of his letter,

a rational man whose one fiction is space,
    and whatever objects patrol
the galaxies, who parked upon our cliff,

observed the red lights of a saucer trace
a weird parabola, and then rebuff
his vision, disappearing through a hole
in the night sky, and as an aftermath

engendering its own fog of escape.
  Nightly, he'd come back to this spot,
and we'd observed his lightless car stationed
at all hours on the cliff, while hoarse seas broke
in the hollow beneath. At dawn, his red
tail-lights would recede like two polka dots
into the grey. And then we'd ascertained

his motives by his writing. Birds were our
    obsession, watching the genus
of gulls, kittiwakes, shearwaters, herring
and black backed gulls, tattle the coast and scour
the beach for food. On the water's bright ring,
we knew each species, and in the wind's flash
their note of outcry, coming and going

with the sea change. And then you, Mr. James,
    were here at dusk with a dossier
of photographs, each irrefutable
to an untutored eye, and sparks of rain
flicked on the windows. By the tea-table
a storm was beating up, and your setter
whined at the bang of thunder, and shelter

was yours for the taking. That night a gull
    flew violently at the window,
and dropped, a deadweight to the ground. I peered
out through the dark, but couldn't mark its fall;
and in the morning it had disappeared,
and not a bird showed on the coast. A hole
was above us; our man was running scared.

# SONGS

## ALLEGORY OF THE WELL

*for David Gascoyne*

Lately I came by a well,
and I saw the sun therein,
emblazoning its eight rays
at a sky black as moleskin,
and beside the well a pail
bid me draw, but then the day
changed upon the midnight bell.

In the noonday I stole back,
and I saw the moon therein,
lucently waxed to the full,
and darkness became the noon,
no star showed in the sky's track;
and I could not use the pail
for I was blinded by black.

So I sat beside that well,
divining when light should come,
and of its strange alchemy,
but a star eclipsed the moon,
and fell down inside the pail.
Neither in the well nor sky
would the sun show through the gale.

And rasping within the storm,
a winged serpent with gold claws
brooded like an owl over
the well, and its arcane laws,
while I watched a sun with horns
challenge a moon with lunar
rays, and a strange egg was born.

From it a jewelled marine-cock
sought the hoopoe in its nest
for its medicinal stone,
and the serpent's scarlet crest
set fire to water and rock;
by that well I stood alone,
gold pebbles littered the track.

# DECEPTIONS ARE APPEARANCES

This man going up the hill
met his own death coming down,
and bypassed the apparition,
and contemptuously threw
stones at it, and left it broken,
stretched out as a crooked shadow.

And went on to the hill's summit,
and felt the absence of his death
lying dead upon the heath,
and descended in vain to search
for who abducted by a thief
mocked him as sustenance for rats.

And met a second stranger who
pointed towards the upas tree,
from which a man undyingly
hung in a cloud, and sang, I'm he
you killed because my legacy
was to become you when you die,

but that you killed your very death
at first sight on that barren path,
showing your malice with such wrath
I turned into a man of wealth,
who outlives life, while you beneath
the earth will know the dark of death.

## HOUSE WITHOUT WALLS

I bid my enemy depart,
he cursed me, and took me for dead,
who lay beneath my fallen house,
and dreamed upon a pallet-bed.
The Tree of Death grew in my head.

And in the leaves I saw his face,
and then a storm beat down that tree,
and in its place my ruined house
was raised, but then my enemy
was in the house and had the key.

I went off and my anger showed,
and grew to a black speaking cloud,
which took me from my own country;
my enemy lay on the road
couched as a dog, I wished him dead.

And where I went my house followed.
I dreamed I died so that I lived,
and when I woke I joined the dead.
My enemy lay down and died,
The Tree of Life grew in my head.

## TREE OF DEATH

I gave my love to a scarlet rose,
it withered to a blackened thorn;
luxuriant green of the oak
reverted to a dead acorn,
leaving us helpless to the storm's
mintage of heavy rain.

The thorn drew blood, and on the ground
it shone as an eight-pointed star,
and when I placed the acorn there,
a warlock child with silver hair
sprang up. We knew the midnight bell
as the last of the year.

You stand beneath the Tree of Death
not Life, the warlock said, and placed
his foot on the circumference
of the enormity the dead
would come to inhabit when raised
upon that plain, naked.

And through the dark we feared to see
horsemen breaking out of each cloud.
We linked arms on our marriage day,
and danced the dance of death in shrouds,
while overhead the moon was blood
red on the risen dead.

# THE KING AND THE SPECTRE

*for Anthony Rudolf*

Out in the noonday dust I saw
an old man wearing a lead crown,
who dragged a spectre on a lead
around the rowan, red rowan.
The spectre's crown was of iron,
and he was of ursine paw.

And who was King, and who was slave,
I couldn't discern, both bore pain
of centuries upon their face,
beneath the rowan, red rowan;
and ugly shadows crossed that plain
and flitted round an open grave.

The two were linked by a gold thread
that was fastened to a grey sun
which stood still as the two divined
beneath the rowan, red rowan,
whether to remain there or run
among the gossamer-fine dead.

But then the spectre shook the tree,
and gibbon-like demons plumped down,
and killed the old man who was King
beneath the rowan, red rowan,
while the spectre wore a gold crown,
and the sun fell out of the sky.

# TREE OF FRIGHT

*for Kathleen Raine*

When I walked into the garden
a black shadow grew from my head,
it grew larger pointing upwards,
and evil birds alighted on
it, and the garden turned to weed.

When I walked into the shadows
it grew light, and pointed downwards
to the weeds, and a serpent weaved
black and white and yellow flowers,
and on its tongue retained a seed.

I balanced this shadow, it grew
divided between dark and light,
dark by day and light by night,
and when the wind blew it was still,
I called it by the name of Fright.

I nurtured it, and it conceived
clouds upon a heavenly tree,
whose black and gold leaves shone brightly,
but then the gold leaves turned to red
and with the black fell from the sky.

My Tree of Fright remained austere;
its spectre disturbed my mind,
and when I walked, menaced the ground;
the serpent had climbed in its bare
branches, and fattened its green rind.